<u>COYOTE THUNDER</u>
One-Act Version

by David Andrew Laws

Dedicated to my teammates – always and especially Alex

with special thanks to Alex Bratton, Maddie Fisette, Leticia Julian, Alex Muhlenkamp, Treasure Nelson, Geoff Pictor, Luke Hampson, Emry Sottile, Xandra Abney, Gregory Petershack, Rebekah Nogueira, Lainee Jentz, Sarah Gordon-Macey, Camille Larsen, Eryn Barnes, Kyra Leeds, Sarah Goldstein, Sarah Davis Reynolds, Sophia Carlin, Alivia Quattrocki, Stephen Solomon, Laura Hall, & Kyle Holmes

LICENSING & PRODUCTION INQUIRIES
Uproar Theatrics, LLC.
hello@uproartheatrics.com | www.UproarTheatrics.com

<u>**SCENES**</u>
Scene One – Thursday, March 15th – MaMaLynn3's Out Sick
Scene Two – Friday, March 16th – Who's Your Captain?
Scene Three – Saturday, March 17th – You Dirty Rat
Scene Four – Sunday, March 18th – The Calm
Scene Five – Monday, March 19th – All Rise
Scene Six – Tuesday, March 20th – Talkin' with turtle-dance™
Scene Seven – Wednesday, March 21st – Walk the Plank
Scene Eight – Thursday, March 22nd – AVM
Scene Nine – Friday, March 23rd – To Be or Not To Be?

<u>**SETTING**</u> – A spare multi-purpose room at West Harris High School in West Harris, Missouri, USA

<u>**CAST**</u> –
The Tank: Grace Hubert aka **h00ba_h00ba** – head first, heart follows; not afraid to take damage; distracts enemies so others can shine – a sophomore

The Healer: Rebecca Ashworth aka **Ashworth1** – keeps you alive; has an eye on everyone's energy; giving, even when it takes from her – a junior

The Captain: Lynne Burton aka **MaMaLynn3** – calls the shots; rallies from every angle; not above a sacrifice play – a senior

The Pusher: Jade Lee aka **fear0000** – knows every trick in the book; excellent at finding pressure points; not afraid to play dirty – a junior

The Scout: Katie Mayfield aka **imcnu4ever** – thinks at the speed of light; delicate but dextrous; saw you coming from a mile away – a sophomore

The Swing: Courtney Williamson aka **turtle-dance** –
observes and absorbs; hasn't made it onto the field yet; jack
of all trades, master of none – a freshman

The Adult: Derrick Cunningham aka **Mr. Derrick** –
voluntold to this position, but does believe in its value;
usually attends more practices, but this week has been crazy;
competent, not confident – mid-thirties

<u>A Note on Casting</u>: In most of my work, I am fairly gender-
agnostic, but The Coyotes need to be girls. Whether they're
high school girls now or were ones once, this is a play for
them, so please put them in it. Diversity is good, and it
would be awesome to see this story represented with a
diverse cast in terms of race, body type, etc. In any case, suit
the actor to the role and the role to the actor.

Mr. Derrick is ideally played by an adult, but can be played
by a student as an adult and/or adjusted to be Mrs. Derrick if
necessary (in which case Derrick would presumably be her
maiden name).

<u>A Note on the Script</u>: The "//" symbol indicates an overlap
in dialogue, i.e. when the next character begins speaking
overtop of the ongoing line. The more conversationally this
dialogue can be presented, the better. It should feel like the
play was not written but recorded from the conversations of
actual high schoolers. If that means changing words,
adjusting timing, or updating slang, so be it. Say it in your
own voice, but tell the story.

Words are <u>underlined</u> for emphasis, either in tempo, volume,
or emotion, i.e. louder, faster, funnier.

Sometimes [brackets] are used to indicate feelings. These are subtextual and should not be represented verbally.

Also, I know a cut of this length is sometimes necessary, but I implore you to at least make the full-length version available to your actors. There is so much nuance and relationship development that just wouldn't fit in a one-act cut. I encourage you to use the original script as a point of reference, a dramaturgical guide, an exercise in character exploration.

Or don't, what am I gonna do, I'm just an author's note.

<u>A Note on Censorship:</u> One of the intentions of this script is to give voice to some weird little freaks. Some real odd ducks. Those who think too much and care too little. Or vice versa. The time in these characters' lives is such a critical one, both internally and externally, and I hope the exploration of these energies onstage can offer actors and audiences a little grace, a little joy, a little hope, a little catharsis, and a lot to consider.

That said, I understand that not everyone loves swear words. Though our most primal expressions – vulgarity, rage, sexuality – are universal, some people prefer those expressions to exist within very specific parameters, and the high school battlefield is not always one of those times or places. Most instances of profanity and vulgarity have been scrubbed from this version of the script, but if there are still moments that you fear might induce too much pearl clutching, reach out and we'll see what adjustments can be made. In any case, in your exploration of these themes, I encourage you to be brave, and even a little weird, as the play teaches us.

<u>**A Note on Names:**</u> Though the characters have "real names", and even refer to one another by them sometimes, The Coyotes should still be credited with their online handles (i.e. starring Dame Judy Dench as MaMaLynn3). When full usernames are said out loud, they are pronounced:

h00ba_h00ba = /ˈhuːbə ˈhuːbə/ or HOO-buh HOO-buh (without pronouncing the underscore)

Ashworth1 = /ˈæʃwɝθ wʌn/ or ASH-wurth-WON

MaMaLynn3 = /ˌmɑmə ˈlɪn/ or MAH-muh-LIN

fear0000 = /fɪəɹ ˈzɪɹoʊ zɪɹoʊ zɪɹoʊ zɪɹoʊ/ or FEER-ZEER-oh-ZEER-oh-ZEER-oh-ZEER-oh (not /fɪˈɹuː/ or /fɪɹ oʊ oʊ oʊ oʊ/)

imcnu4ever = /aɪ ɛm siː ɛn ju fɔɹˈɛvɚ/ or AYE-em-SEE-en-YOU-for-EV-er
or cnu = /siː ɛn juː/ or SEE-en-YOU

turtle-dance = /ˈtɝtəl ˌdæns/ or TUR-tl-DANSS (without pronouncing the hyphen)

<u>**SCENE ONE – THURSDAY – MAMALYNN3'S OUT
SICK**</u>

*Pre-show, the room is dark, lit by the ambient
lighting of electronics, perhaps decorated with
LED strips and other paraphernalia that allude
to the "gamer" aesthetic. We can't see a lot of
this in the dark, but we are in a multi-purpose
room in a high school, and it's got some
personality. Posters, wear and tear, mementos –
this is one of those spaces that gets taken over
by the students. They treat it as well as they're
going to, but you can tell it's been theirs for a
while.*

*There is a door into the room SR. In moments of
realism, entrances are made through the SR
door, but more heightened moments do not live
by this constraint and characters can come from
anywhere.*

*Centerstage are six desks together as one unit,
each outfitted with a full gaming PC set-up:
chair, tower, monitor, keyboard, mouse, over-the-
ear-headphones, the works. The stations are
somewhat uniform, but there are little
personalizations at each: a forgotten water
bottle, a good luck charm, a snack wrapper,
discarded assignments, etc. Again, the room has
been used, lived in, not literally but emotionally
– the battlestations onstage reflect the essence of
the dressing rooms backstage. Their ownership
is, in order clockwise from SR, turtle-dance,
h00ba_h00ba, imcnu4ever, MaMaLynn3,
Ashworth1, fear0000.*

*The moment before is calm. Everything is
happening elsewhere in the building. Then, at*

*start, lights and sound blast off. It's a stadium
intro with fog and confetti and whatever else is
available. At first, we just hear music. We're
getting excited, we're getting pumped. Then,
h00ba_h00ba, Ashworth1, fear0000,
imcnu4ever, and turtle-dance enter. It should be
a big scenic moment but it's…sloppy. Ad-libbed.
Almost reads as something's gone wrong. They
weren't ready.*

*They carry backpacks, books, whatever they
would have had with them at the end of the day.
turtle-dance has a microphone but she's too
nervous to use it, doesn't know what to say,
doesn't know what The Coyotes want her to do.
imcnu4ever, h00ba_h00ba, fear0000, and
Ashworth1 cajole her, corral her, trying to pump
her up to pump up the crowd, but she's just not
getting it. The noise and music of the intro mask
most of what they're saying, but we catch
snippets of her fear and their frustration and
encouragement. Eventually, fear0000 snatches
the mic from turtle-dance [watch and learn] and
takes centerstage.*

fear0000
(as an announcer, really drawing out the name)
Iiiiiiiintroducing Coyotteeeeeeee Thunnndderrrrrrr!

*(The audience's cheers and applause are
bolstered by the sound design. fear0000 soaks it
in, an expert emcee. imcnu4ever, h00ba_h00ba,
and Ashworth1 put their things at their stations
and watch proudly from the wings, upstage,
wherever. turtle-dance watches too, separate,
embarrassed and a little confused.)*

fear0000

Todaaaaayyy's grudge match is a best-of-three, double-elimination, weapons-only pressure gauntlet against their longtime rivals, The Lewisburrrg Liooonnnns!

> *(The audience is allowed time to react again.
> The sound design leads with boos and jeers as
> well as a few cheers from fans of the visiting
> team.)*

fear0000

And you know what game we're playing today, folks! The heart-stoppin'-est, overclockin'-est, lootin', shootin', jumbo-bootin'-est…your favorite MOBA and mine, BONEBLOOD ARENA TWOOOOO!!

> *(The reaction to this is devastatingly excited.
> Everybody loves this game and its hyper-
> competitive community.)*

fear0000

(brings it down; makes 'em lean in) Now. We know you love the players as much as you love the game, so let's make some noise for the ladies of LAN, the queens of the quest marker, the DPS divas. COYYOOOTEEEE THUNNDERRRR!

> *(h00ba_h00ba, imcnu4ever, and Ashworth1 join
> fear0000. They are howling – chanting, woofing,
> chest bumping, high-fiving – howling. turtle-
> dance follows physically but does not know how
> to participate.*
>
> *After they celebrate, h00ba_h00ba, imcnu4ever,
> and Ashworth1 wait like greyhounds in the slip.
> As each Coyote's handle is announced, the name
> can appear in the space through whatever*

*means available: lights, projections, extras
holding up placards that spell them out, etc.)*

fear0000

First on the field is a precision fighter who needs no
introduction – but we're gonna give it to her anyway – put
your hands together for your Pusher: fear zero zero zero
zerooooooo! *(off-mic)* Oh wait, that's me!

*(fear0000 takes center, shadowboxes and
finishes with a big kick, really soaking up the
attention.)*

fear0000

Next up – you'll never see her coming, but she's always got
her eye on you. It's your Scout: i m c n u 4 everrrrr!

*(imcnu4ever does a combat roll to center, hops
up, and scopes out the room with her hand
above her eyes. She recognizes the audience's
presence [oh! didn't see you there], and basks it
in. She then takes the mic from fear0000 who
goes to her station, puts on her headphones, and
starts to play.)*

imcnu4ever

Uh oh! Here comes a knockout in more ways than one. She
takes a beating and keeps on competing – give it up for your
Tank, h00ba h000000baaaaa!

*(h00ba_h00ba takes center, drops and does
some show-offy push-ups, then pops up for the
mic handoff. imcnu4ever goes to her station,
puts on her headphones, and starts to play.)*

h00ba_h00ba

You can't live with her, and you <u>won't</u> live long without her.
Let's hear it for your Healer: Ashworth one!

> *(Ashworth1 takes center with a bow, blows the
> audience a kiss, a wink, a little wave, then takes
> the mic from h00ba_h00ba who goes to her
> station, puts on her headphones, and starts to
> play.*
>
> *With this, the time has come, and the room
> knows it. If rhythmic stomping and clapping is
> going to commence, this is where it starts
> underscoring. Ashworth1 summons turtle-dance
> who approaches center timidly. Ashworth1
> passes turtle-dance the mic [you got this], then
> goes to her station, puts on her headphones, and
> starts to play. turtle-dance takes in the crowd,
> breathes, and speaks. She is not as proficient as
> the other Coyotes, but the microphone helps,
> and she gets into it by the end.)*

turtle-dance

Annnnnd last but absolutely never least, it's time to say *(with
a little howl; she's trying but her heart's not in it)* hellooooo
to Coyote Thunder's den mother. The queen of the screen.
The MVP of the PVP. The…North Star of the…health bar….

> *(turtle-dance glances back to see how she's
> doing. Ashworth1 [you're doing great, keep
> going], fear0000 [boo, that stinked],
> h00ba_h00ba [get on with it already], and
> imcnu4ever [eh, that was okay] give her various
> hand signals of encouragement without looking
> up from their screens. turtle-dance turns back
> and continues to do her best.)*

turtle-dance

Please welcome your Captain, MaMaaaaaaLyyyyyynne!!!

> *(imcnu4ever stands up at her station,
> headphones off, phone in hand. Sound stops. Not
> a record scratch, just an emptiness.)*

imcnu4ever

(simply; reporting) Oh wait, never mind. MaMaLynn3's not
coming.

turtle-dance *(overlapping)* What?
Ashworth1 *(overlapping)* What do you mean?
h00ba_h00ba *(overlapping; lifting a headphone from her
ear)* Who's not what?
fear0000 *(overlapping; died in the game)* Aw, h00ba, pay
attention!

imcnu4ever

(getting the news from her phone) She just texted – she went
home early cause she's got a migraine. Practice is cancelled.

> *(The natural lights come on, all of the ceremony
> is gone. It's not a stadium anymore, it's just a
> spare room in a high school, fluorescent and
> dull.)*

turtle-dance

Oh.

> *(h00ba_h00ba rips off her headphones in
> frustration.)*

h00ba_h00ba

Son of a–

Ashworth1

Will she be back tomorrow?

fear0000

Oh my god, they're gonna kick our <u>dumpers</u> this weekend.

h00ba_h00ba

(packing up; choosing to be unbothered) Whatever, those guys suck. They're the same old stupid Lewisburg <u>boys'</u> club they've always been.

imcnu4ever

Not anymore; they got a new Pusher.

fear0000

What?? Who??

Ashworth1

What'sa matter, fear? Scared of the new blood?

fear0000

(facetious and defensive) Please, I'm <u>made</u> of blood. My body's, like, seventy percent blood.

turtle-dance

I think you're thinking of water.

fear0000

(to turtle-dance) Don't ever presume to know what I'm thinking.

imcnu4ever

I don't know her name but apparently she's a ringer.

fear0000

(terrified; mortified; furious; intrigued) "She??"

(h00ba_h00ba and Ashworth1 look at each other with shock and delight, then at fear0000, then back at each other.)

fear0000

(at h00ba_h00ba and Ashworth1) Shut up. *(back to imcnu4ever)* Who said?

imcnu4ever

They made a post; it was a whole big thing. Do you guys not follow them?

(The Coyotes' response is starkly casual, a massive shift from the intros.)

fear0000 *(overlapping)* Why would I? Stupid. Whatever.
Ashworth1 *(overlapping)* My phone's acting weird, I might need a new one.
h00ba_h00ba *(overlapping)* …I'm grounded from my phone.

fear0000

Who cares?? If we're not practicing, we're as good as we're gonna get; let's go home. We'll roll up on Saturday to click butt and take names.

h00ba_h00ba

(just hyper at this point) Yeah! Who needs practice?

imcnu4ever

(annoyed; [that's enough]) Alright.

fear0000

MaMaLynn3's just given us a snow day, and we're all stupid for not being at home in our pjs right now.

imcnu4ever

This is not time off. *(checking her phone)* She says to run drills at home and that she will be back tomorrow. And tomorrow–

Ashworth1

(quoting Macbeth; very dramatic) "...and tomorrow, and tomorrow…"

> *(The other Coyotes give Ashworth1 a weird look.)*

Ashworth1

You guys haven't done your Shakespeare assignment at <u>all</u>, have you? // It's due next week.

fear0000

(smilingly nastily) Man, <u>screw</u> MaMaLynn3, I hope she <u>never</u> comes back.

imcnu4ever

(like a chained dog) Hey!!!

> *(The other Coyotes react to imcnu4ever's sudden ferocity.)*

imcnu4ever

<u>Don't</u>…say that about her.

> *(h00ba_h00ba looks to fear0000 and rolls her eyes.)*

fear0000

(as genuine as she can be) Relax. It was just a joke.

imcnu4ever
She's your Captain, so she's in charge. And that's no joke.

Ashworth1
Look, it's been a long day. *(trying to find common ground)* I don't know if you guys had that sub in // Geometry, but he was a real creep.

fear0000
(overlapping) Ohhhh, I did.

h00ba_h00ba
(overlapping; suggestively) He did not seem like a sub to me. But I could <u>make</u> him one.

Ashworth1
Ew.

h00ba_h00ba
That's "Ew, <u>mistress</u>."

fear0000
(to h00ba_h00ba; only mostly joking) It is really hard to be your friend sometimes.

> *(h00ba_h00ba puts a hand on fear0000's shoulder.)*

h00ba_h00ba
(saccharine) We're not friends. We're teammates.

Ashworth1
(to fear0000) Do you have something to say to your <u>other</u> teammate?

*(Ashworth1 steers fear0000 toward imcnu4ever.
imcnu4ever is still upset but trying to hide it.
fear0000 is annoyed but acquiesces.)*

fear0000

Look, I'm sorry I ragged on MaMaLynn3, okay? I know you
guys are close. She and I are just…not, so… *(hands raised in
surrender)* I'll do extra drills tonight to make up for it.

imcnu4ever

Just…don't let her hear you talk that way, okay? She's your
Captain and she deserves your respect.

fear0000

(grabbing her bag) Yeah, well, why don'tcha marry her if
you love her so much? *(going to leave)* Later, nerds!

turtle-dance

(of MaMaLynn3; cutting through in its simplicity of thought)
If she's not coming, should I play?

*(This stops fear0000 half-in and half-out of the
doorway and catches h00ba_h00ba, Ashworth1,
and imcnu4ever off guard. [awkward])*

imcnu4ever

(referencing her phone) I mean, Lynne said practice is
cancelled.

turtle-dance

I know but, like, I'm The Swing, so. I'm supposed to fill in?

Ashworth1

(diplomatic) I think that's only for…

fear0000 *(overlapping)* emergencies.

h00ba_h00ba *(overlapping)* worst-case scenarios.

Ashworth1

Like a competition.

fear0000 *(overlapping)* Or the rapture.
h00ba_h00ba *(overlapping)* Diarrhea.

turtle-dance

But, how does that make sense? Don't I need to practice with you guys?

fear0000

You watch us, don't you?

turtle-dance

Yeah, but that's not the same as <u>actually</u> playing together.

h00ba_h00ba

You gotta use your imaaaginnattion, turtle-pants.

fear0000

(under her breath) Not her strong suit.

turtle-dance

What?

Ashworth1

(mediating; to imcnu4ever) Let's bring it up to MaMaLynn3 that turtle-dance needs some practice time. *(trying to rekindle the group)* <u>Afterrrrr</u> we kick the butts off of The Lions, yeah??

> *(This rallies h00ba_h00ba and fear0000 into leaving, chatting as they go. Ashworth1 joins*

them. imcnu4ever starts to pack but isn't with them.)

h00ba_h00ba

(nudging fear0000) Try not to think about the new Pusher's butt too much, fear.

fear0000

Just because I'm the only one that's <u>out</u> doesn't mean I'm the only queer here. *(fingers pointing from her eyes to turtle-dance)* Keepin' an eye on <u>you</u>, turtle.

imcnu4ever

Let's get logged in at home. Drills are not optional!

h00ba_h00ba

(chanting) Drills, drills, drills, drills!

(Ashworth1, fear0000, and h00ba_h00ba are gone. imcnu4ever and turtle-dance linger in a brief, awkward silence.)

imcnu4ever

We <u>will</u> make sure you get some practice. Now's just…not the right time to be…mixing things up. Too many unknowns.

turtle-dance

I get it. *(trying to make a point)* But she's gonna graduate in, like, two months. // If she's–

imcnu4ever

Yeah, that's *(doesn't want to think about it)* a while away. And for the record, you're still a freshman. You've got a long way to go to prove yourself.

turtle-dance

How can I do that if–?

imcnu4ever

(cutting her off) I don't wanna argue. I just wanna do what MaMaLynn3 says while MaMaLynn3's in charge. Okay?

turtle-dance

(out of ammunition) Okay.

imcnu4ever

Practice tomorrow, game on Saturday. We'll talk about scheduling you time after that. In the meantime–

turtle-dance

(glumly [i get it]) Drills. And respect the hierarchy.

imcnu4ever

You catch on quick.

> *(imcnu4ever exits. turtle-dance watches her go, then looks back at the battlestations. For a moment, she considers smashing them all. The lights redden gradually as we watch her standing in silence, imagining picking up a bat and laying waste to the unfair system. We hear her grunts of effort and the crashing of electronics as she remains still and breathing, envisioning the simple destruction. The sound stops when Mr. Derrick opens the door and ducks his head in. Her focus remains on the battlestations.)*

Mr. Derrick

Hey, ladies, MaMaLynn3 is– *(realizing it's just turtle-dance)* op! Where's everybody?

turtle-dance

(simply; reporting) MaMaLynn3's got a migraine, so they all left. We're gonna do drills at home.

Mr. Derrick

(that's what he came to tell them [okay, cool]) Then my work here is done. Have a good night, Courtney. Get home safe.

turtle-dance

You too.

> *(Mr. Derrick exits, closing the door behind him.*
> *turtle-dance stands alone for a moment.*
> *Blackout.)*

SCENE TWO – FRIDAY – WHO'S YOUR CAPTAIN?

The lights come up on The Coyotes at their stations, mid-practice. They are headphone mic'd up and intensely focused. MaMaLynn3, h00ba_h00ba, imcnu4ever, fear0000, and Ashworth1 are playing. turtle-dance is spectating.

The atmosphere is that of a war room – a green tint, severity and meticulous planning. The soundscape of their game – lasers, explosions, and monsters dying – is far more epic than the reality of them sitting behind computer screens. Their voices are distorted like they're running a military operation.

MaMaLynn3

On me, on me.

imcnu4ever

South sector is clear.

h00ba_h00ba

You guys gotta go–

(The Coyotes lapse into furious typing and clicking, except for turtle-dance who merely spectates.)

Ashworth1

Crap– Contact!

MaMaLynn3

Gotta what?

fear0000

Flanking left.

MaMaLynn3

h00ba, report back.

h00ba_h00ba

I need // med up!

Ashworth1

Covered.

MaMaLynn3

h00ba!

h00ba_h00ba

Moving.

MaMaLynn3

Negative, not–

fear0000

Turret neutralized.

h00ba_h00ba

Target in range.

MaMaLynn3

fear, can you–

Ashworth1

I'm on your six.

h00ba_h00ba

In position.

imcnu4ever

North sector clear.

MaMaLynn3

I repeat, negative–

fear0000

Take the shot!

MaMaLynn3

h00ba!!

imcnu4ever

All sectors clear!

fear0000

TAKE THE SHOT!!

> *(h00ba_h00ba takes the shot. We hear a ringing explosion and the sound of victory. The military aspects of the scene fade into a naturalistic neutrality. h00ba_h00ba rips her headphones off in celebration and cheers. fear0000 takes off her headphones and high-fives h00ba_h00ba. MaMaLynn3 snaps her headphones off in frustration. Ashworth1 and imcnu4ever remove their headphones calmly. turtle-dance remains headphones on, observing the screen.*
>
> *MaMaLynn3 stands and pushes her chair down away from the battlestation. She rushes on h00ba_h00ba.)*

MaMaLynn3

(pointing at fear0000) Is she your Captain?

h00ba_h00ba

No, but–

MaMaLynn3

No buts! Is she your Captain?

fear0000

Lynne, calm–

imcnu4ever

(to fear0000) Don't.

> *(h00ba_h00ba stands up to face MaMaLynn3.
> Even if she doesn't physically tower over
> MaMaLynn3, it feels like she does.)*

h00ba_h00ba

She's not my Captain. But I didn't take the shot because she told me to, I took the shot because <u>you</u> didn't. I saw an opportunity–

MaMaLynn3

It was out of line!

fear0000

What's the big deal?

Ashworth1

Yeah, MaMaLynn3, it's okay. We still won.

MaMaLynn3

(looping the whole team into the chastisement) <u>First</u> of all, we won against <u>bots</u>. If that'd been The Lions, they totally would have blocked the shot and had us on the defensive. Our defense is weak–

h00ba_h00ba

Because <u>you</u> skipped practice yesterday.

MaMaLynn3

–<u>because</u> last night's patch nerfed the shield gun and we haven't had time to adjust our plays.

imcnu4ever

Which means The Lions haven't either.

fear0000

This isn't our first pressure gauntlet. We didn't need–

MaMaLynn3

It's not about "<u>need</u>!" It's about <u>can</u> we or <u>can't</u> we? Are we a team, or are we just players?

h00ba_h00ba

Well, what about you?? You missed <u>four</u> shots on that ultra-goblin before you finally connected. // Feelin' rusty after your day off?

MaMaLynn3

That's because I was trying to– It was not a day <u>off</u>, first of all. Second of all, I was distracted by your *(mocking)* "You guys gotta go" that <u>you</u> wouldn't explain.

h00ba_h00ba

I didn't have time to explain.

MaMaLynn3

YOU HAVE TO MAKE TIME TO EXPLAIN. YOU HAVE TO COMMUNICATE.

fear0000

(drenched in sarcasm) Calm down, Lynne, you're gonna give yourself another migraine.

MaMaLynn3 *(overlapping)* Shut up, fear.
Ashworth1 *(overlapping)* fear, too far.
imcnu4ever *(overlapping)* That's not funny, fear! But, Lynne, you should–

h00ba_h00ba

Man, whatever. I don't need this. I'm gonna play how I'm gonna play, and if you don't like it, you can take it up with me in the gauntlet. *(goes to grab her things)* I'll see you guys in the arena tomorrow.

MaMaLynn3

Maybe you won't.

> *(MaMaLynn3 freezes. The whole scene freezes. The mood, accompanied by the lighting, shifts. There's a dust in the air. It is high noon.)*

h00ba_h00ba

(without turning around) What'd you say?

MaMaLynn3

(smugly) Maybe you won't see us in the arena tomorrow. Maybe turtle-dance will.

> *(Suddenly, it's a Western. A classic "oo-wee-oo-wee-oo" whistle and a "wah wah wahhhhh" sound. Everything is moving through molasses as h00ba_h00ba turns back. turtle-dance finally realizes something's going on, takes off her headphones.)*

turtle-dance

Hey, I was just watching the playback, and–

h00ba_h00ba

(to MaMaLynn3; with a thick cowboy accent) Are you threatenin' me, you lily-livered son of a gun?

> *(h00ba_h00ba puts on a ten gallon hat. MaMaLynn3 matches h00ba_h00ba's cowboy posturing.)*

MaMaLynn3

(with an even thicker cowboy accent) Maybe I am. Maybe I ain't. Whatchu gonna do about it?

> *(MaMaLynn3, Ashworth1, imcnu4ever, and fear0000 also each don a ten gallon hat.)*

turtle-dance

Wwwwwwhat did I miss?

MaMaLynn3

This town ain't big enough for your britches, h00ba_h00ba.

> *(h00ba_h00ba moves her hands to her hips, hovering them over two invisible holsters. MaMaLynn3 does the same.)*

h00ba_h00ba

(glaring at MaMaLynn3) I reckon this's been a long time comin' 'tween you and me.

MaMaLynn3

I reckon so too.

h00ba_h00ba

I reckoned you might reckon so too. I reckon.

MaMaLynn3

Enough reckonin'! State yer terms.

h00ba_h00ba

You're fast on that keyboard. Let's see how well you do offline, you buzzard-lovin' scoundrel.

MaMaLynn3

On three?

h00ba_h00ba

I wouldn't have it any other way.

MaMaLynn3

One.

h00ba_h00ba

Two.

MaMaLynn3

Th–

> *(h00ba_h00ba has already "drawn" her "gun" [it's just her hand] when Mr. Derrick enters, deflating the moment and restoring the atmosphere to normal. He has an open letter in hand. The Coyotes' heads all pivot at the intrusion, then h00ba_h00ba turns back to MaMaLynn3.)*

h00ba_h00ba

Screw you, Lynne.

*(h00ba_h00ba disengages, and The Coyotes
settle, turning their attention to what Mr.
Derrick has to say.)*

Mr. Derrick

(doesn't mind, but it <u>is</u> his job) Alright, well, language. But,
hey, huddle up, friends. Got some news!

fear0000

We're not gonna huddle up, Mr. Derrick. Just tell us.

Mr. Derrick

(trying not to let teenage girls make him cry again)
Alllllllright. Well, exciting development for tomorrow's
game against The Lions. A talent scout will be there!
Someone from… *(checking the letter)* Maryville. *(checks
again)* University. Apparently they might be interested in
offering someone on the winning team some kind of
scholarship.

*(The Coyotes absorb this information with a
variety of wide eyes and slack jaws.)*

Mr. Derrick

(when no one responds) But, uh….

*(h00ba_h00ba, fear0000, Ashworth1,
MaMaLynn3, and imcnu4ever explode into a
primal rage. The sun has gone down, and
they're not sure it will ever return. Drums
accompany their frenzy, and the lighting makes
the room look dark yet ominous, like the glow
from an active volcano. They are not indicative
of any real or perceived cultures; they are purely
unga bunga. turtle-dance retreats to Mr.
Derrick's side, who watches as if this is perfectly
normal.)*

h00ba_h00ba

h00ba <u>eat</u> talent scout!

Ashworth1

h00ba no eat!! Ashworth SMASH!

fear0000

NO EAT, NO SMASH, FEAR SET HIM ON FIRE!!!

>*(imcnu4ever gets up on something, a chair or a desk, and MaMaLynn3, Ashworth1, h00ba_h00ba, and fear0000 gaze up at her.)*

imcnu4ever

MaMaLynn3 is leader! MaMaLynn3 speaks for Coyotes!!

>*(Ashworth1, h00ba_h00ba, and fear0000 snarl and gnash as imcnu4ever pulls MaMaLynn3 up to the elevated position and then takes her place below with the others.)*

imcnu4ever

(encouraging her) MaMaLynn3 speak.

>*(MaMaLynn3 accepts once more the burden of leadership with a soft-spoken dignity.)*

MaMaLynn3

Coyotes work hard. Play hard. Coyotes make plan. Work together. Coyotes together <u>strong</u>.

>*(fear0000, h00ba_h00ba, imcnu4ever, and Ashworth1 grunt and nod in agreement. This is riling them up in a good way)*

h00ba_h00ba
What do, MaMaLynn3?? What do??

MaMaLynn3
(laying out the plan like a ritual) First, Ashworth smash.
(more gleeful agreement) <u>Then</u> fear set on fire. *(the joy rises)*
<u>Then</u>, h00ba eat! And Coyotes win!

>	*(imcnu4ever, h00ba_h00ba, Ashworth1, and
>	fear0000 celebrate their theoretical victory.)*

MaMaLynn3
Then h00ba poop him out and smash him again! Then eat
him again, then set him on fire again. Whatever it take for
Coyotes to be NUMBER ONE!!

>	*(imcnu4ever, h00ba_h00ba, Ashworth1, and
>	fear0000 repeat "NUMBER ONE!!" and howl
>	heroically, devotees before a bloodthirsty god.)*

Mr. Derrick
(teacher voice a little; just getting over the din) Okay, cool
but, ladies–

>	*(The atmosphere and The Coyotes return to
>	normal.)*

Mr. Derrick
(as if they'd just been talking about video games) You can't
do any of that here. Not tonight anyway. Practice is over. The
building's closing.

MaMaLynn3
(exhales; still shaking off the fervor) Fine! Can you just…
give us a sec?

Mr. Derrick

Y'okie dokie.

> *(Mr. Derrick leaves, closing the door behind him.)*

MaMaLynn3

Can you all get on tonight?

fear0000 *(overlapping)* Pssh, it's Friday night, I can do whatever I want.
Ashworth1 *(overlapping)* Lemme, uh…yeah, I can. I'll make something up.
imcnu4ever *(overlapping)* I'm closest, so I'll host when I get there.
h00ba_h00ba *(overlapping)* Hell yeah, brother.

turtle-dance

Do you still want me there to spectate, or…?

> *(MaMaLynn3 approaches turtle-dance and takes her by the shoulders. She's kind of gassing her up, motivated by the recent news, but she's doing her duty as a good leader.)*

MaMaLynn3

I need you spectating <u>more</u> than <u>ever</u>, turtle-dance. *(turns to the other Coyotes)* Watch these Coyotes like a hawk. We're gonna start with a practice match and up the difficulty until our fingers ache. <u>Everyone's</u> weaknesses are getting tested.

fear0000

That's not fair; h00ba has so many more weaknesses than the rest of us.

h00ba_h00ba

Hey!

MaMaLynn3

(to turtle-dance) Don't let <u>anyone</u> get away with giving less than their best. *(releases her grip)* Coyotes. Dismissed!

> *(The Coyotes disperse to gather their things, chatting as they do.)*

imcnu4ever

A scholarship's the dream. *(to MaMaLynn3)* Do you think we can do it?

MaMaLynn3

More than that; I <u>know</u> we can. *(to the group)* Alright, Coyotes, get home and get logged in. It's gonna be a long night. Oh, and h00ba?

> *(h00ba_h00ba stops and looks at MaMaLynn3. MaMaLynn3 grins and pulls her finger guns from their holsters.)*

MaMaLynn3

(cowboy accent) It ain't over between us, partner. Pww pww.

> *(MaMaLynn3 mimes firing her finger guns at h00ba_h00ba. h00ba_h00ba casually takes both shots, one in each shoulder, and tips an invisible hat at MaMaLynn3. h00ba_h00ba turns toward the door, rears an imaginary horse, making a whinny sound as she does.)*

h00ba_h00ba

(spurring her unseen horse) Hyah!

*(h00ba_h00ba leads a gallop out of the room
and exits. Ashworth1, fear0000, MaMaLynn3,
and imcnu4ever spur their own imaginary
horses and exit after her. turtle-dance shakes her
head and smiles, walking behind them to exit.
Blackout.)*

<u>SCENE THREE – SATURDAY – YOU DIRTY RAT</u>

> *Lights fade up. A moment of stillness before The Coyotes burst through the door in celebration. While not as choreographed as their earlier entrance, they are hooping and hollering all the same.*
>
> *h00ba_h00ba, fear0000, and Ashworth1 enter first. turtle-dance and imcnu4ever follow. MaMaLynn3 enters last and lingers in the doorway.*

h00ba_h00ba

That's what I'm <u>talking</u> about!

fear0000

Lewisburg Lions? More like <u>Loser</u>burg Lions!

Ashworth1

More like Lewisburg lyin' down to take a nap!

h00ba_h00ba

A dirt nap!

turtle-dance

You guys were great!

fear0000

(teasing but also seeking approval) Were we good little girls for MaMaLynn3? We followed your lead.

MaMaLynn3

You did. And I hope you're all proud of yourselves. We really showed 'em what Coyote Thunder's all about!

*(MaMaLynn3, imcnu4ever, fear0000,
h00ba_h00ba, and Ashworth1 howl and
celebrate.)*

h00ba_h00ba *(overlapping; to MaMaLynn3)* When you
taunted that ghoul into picking off the other Tank? Ah! I
thought I was gonna pee myself–
Ashworth1 *(overlapping; to fear0000)* That head-to-head
between you and the other Pusher? *(chef's kiss)* Hall of
Fame-worthy–
MaMaLynn3 *(overlapping; to fear0000)* Two words: Ultra.
Synergy. // We gotta put that footage on the–
fear0000 *(overlapping; to MaMaLynn3)* It's a lot easier
since the patch. But hey, you know what they say–
imcnu4ever *(overlapping; to h00ba_h00ba)* We have <u>got</u> to
get you a new mouse; I could hear every–

turtle-dance

(overtop; simply) So, not to sound like a broken record but…
when do I get to play?

> *(This silences The Coyotes. They can't decide*
> *where to look – at each other, at turtle-dance, at*
> *nothing. turtle-dance asking "…when do I get to*
> *play?" echoes, skipping each time like a*
> *scratched record.)*

MaMaLynn3

I just…need a little more time to strategize, sorry. These
migraines have been kicking my ass.

turtle-dance

But, like…tomorrow? Next week? I want to be the best
teammate I can be, but I can't do that if I don't know what it
feels like to ready up with you guys. Let me run a
scrimmage. A tutorial match. Something!

fear0000

Keep your thong on, squeaky wheel! You'll get your turn.

turtle-dance

When?

fear0000

After.

turtle-dance

After what?

fear0000

After after, man! Don't make me quote *The Karate Kid* at you!

h00ba_h00ba

(a la James Cagney) You dirty rat!

fear0000

That's not *The Karate Kid*!

Ashworth1

Like, not even a little!

h00ba_h00ba

(still a 1930s gangster) Oh, wha'd'you know, ya two-bit palooka?

> *(h00ba_h00ba dons a fedora pulled low over her forehead. Suddenly, the whole room is a black-and-white film stained with cigarette smoke. h00ba_h00ba, MaMaLynn3, Ashworth1, imcnu4ever, and fear0000 are all mobsters. They mime cigars, some of them have finger guns.)*

Ashworth1

Now look here, see? The kid needs time to bake or she's gonna hit her first match like a bug on a windshield.

fear0000

You're all wet! I say we throw her in with the fishes and see if she sleeps or swims.

MaMaLynn3

It's my call, and I'll say when she's gonna get what's comin' to her, see?

h00ba_h00ba

Get what's comin' to her or 'get what's comin' to her'?

MaMaLynn3

(slyly) You'll have to wait and see, see?

turtle-dance

No, I'd…actually like some clarity on that–

fear0000

If she's comin' in, that means one of us is goin' out, see? And if I'm goin' out, I'm takin' one-a yous with me!

> *(Suddenly, it's a standoff! The music is tense. The Coyote gangsters all lift their finger guns at one another. turtle-dance ducks as if there might be real danger, then realizes and feels silly. The other Coyotes swing their finger guns from person to person. h00ba_h00ba swings hers over to fear0000.)*

h00ba_h00ba

If anyone's goin' down, sistah, it's gonna be you!

Ashworth1

(swinging her fingers on h00ba_h00ba) Easy there, big fella. Let's not make any messes you can't mop up after.

imcnu4ever

(swinging one finger at h00ba_h00ba and the other at Ashworth1) Ain't nobody but nobody gonna tell MaMaLynn3 what to do, see?

fear0000

(swinging her finger guns wildly around from person to person) Somebody better start talkin' soon, or you're <u>all</u> gonna be more full of holes than a moldy swiss cheese!!

> *(turtle-dance jumps in the middle of everyone. Her finger guns are SMGs.)*

turtle-dance

I just want to know when it's my turn to play a video game with my <u>little</u> friiiiiieeeeennnnnds!

> *(As she holds out the word "friends," turtle-dance 'fires' her finger guns in every direction. The other Coyotes leap out of the way, hiding behind furniture, in the wings, wherever they can to get away from the destruction. Sound and light intensify this moment, pinging 'bullets' off the walls and floors and such. As turtle-dance runs out of ammo and steam, she lowers her hands and her head, panting heavily. The other Coyotes crawl out of hiding.)*

MaMaLynn3

Okay. Next week it is. Any volunteers to sub out?

(h00ba_h00ba, Ashworth1, fear0000, and imcnu4ever kinda shrug and kick their feet as they respond.)

h00ba_h00ba *(overlapping)* Fine, as long as she doesn't get fingerprints on my monitor.
Ashworth1 *(overlapping)* Happy to step aside for an afternoon; I've got other work to do.
fear0000 *(overlapping)* Whatever, man, maybe I'll take the whole day off while I'm at it.
imcnu4ever *(overlapping)* Of course, MaMaLynn3, whatever you need. No problem.

MaMaLynn3

Great. *(to turtle-dance)* Monday's practice. You're up. We'll start you on Scout. *(to imcnu4ever)* Thanks, cnu.

(imcnu4ever nods. MaMaLynn3 grabs her backpack and starts for the door. She puts a hand on turtle-dance's shoulder.)

MaMaLynn3

And watch it with the "friend" stuff. I get the *Scarface* reference, but. We're not friends, we're teammates.

(h00ba_h00ba puts her hand on fear0000's shoulder and makes a face; a callback to this moment from Scene One. The other Coyotes gather their things, interacting with turtle-dance as they cross to exit through the SR door.)

Ashworth1

No pressure. You're gonna be great.

fear0000

That's really your only option. That or death.

h00ba_h00ba

That or shame! <u>And</u> <u>then</u> <u>death</u>!

imcnu4ever

Don't listen to them. Scout's easy anyway.

MaMaLynn3

See you Monday, Coyote.

imcnu4ever

(almost out the door together) Lynne, can we…talk?

MaMaLynn3

Yeah, what's up?

> *(With the other Coyotes gone, turtle-dance*
> *stands alone for a moment, then smiles in self-*
> *satisfaction. She raises her finger guns together,*
> *blows over the barrels [the tips of her fingers].*
> *Blackout.)*

SCENE FOUR – SUNDAY – THE CALM

> *The lights come up. The room is lit for twenty-four seconds. The lights go down.*
>
> *{author's note: This transition can be cut for time}*

<u>**SCENE FIVE – MONDAY – ALL RISE**</u>

>*The lights come up, or possibly just a spot on h00ba_h00ba as she enters. She is wearing Aviators and standing at attention.*

h00ba_h00ba

All rise! This court is now in session. The honourable Judge MaMa presiding.

>*(Some sort of take on 'Rule, Britannia!' plays as MaMaLynn3, in a British Parliament-style wig and robe, takes her position as judge. Her placement should be as high and centralized as possible, ideally behind a large podium.*
>
>*Downstage of her, fear0000 and Ashworth1 enter on one side as the prosecution, settling into their space. imcnu4ever and turtle-dance, as defense attorney and plaintiff respectively, enter and situate on the other side.*
>
>*MaMaLynn3 bangs her gavel a few times.)*

MaMaLynn3

(with just a <u>horrific</u> British dialect) Ordah! Ordah! I will have ordah in this court!! Ordah, I say!

turtle-dance

MaMaLynn3, no one's saying any–

MaMaLynn3

(with another gavel bang) That's more than enough out of you! It's been an eventful twenty-four hours, and we've <u>much</u> to discuss. So, prosecution, begin your case.

(Ashworth1 steps forward, clears her throat, and begins her opening argument.)

Ashworth1

(lawyerly, but not British) Your honour. As you know, The Lewisburg Lions have challenged us to a rematch. They claim that, at Saturday's match, their Healer was suffering from an unexpected glare on his screen.

MaMaLynn3

(considering) Indeed.

Ashworth1

Furthermore, they assert that their Swing, Tom Friel, communicated this impediment to <u>our</u> Swing, but that this message was not properly relayed from that point on.

turtle-dance

(defensive, almost pleading) I told Mr. Derrick!

fear0000

Objection!

MaMaLynn3

(gavel bang) Ordah!!

fear0000

Your honour, Derrick is about as competent as a bronze-tier training bot.

MaMaLynn3

(considering once more) …you have a point.

imcnu4ever

Your honour, if I may.

(MaMaLynn3 indicates that imcnu4ever may.)

imcnu4ever

My client's lapse in judgement is irrelevant. The matter at hand is the rematch. We already beat The Lions once. <u>Now</u>, they're demanding a do-over because they know something they think we don't. They want to prove that they can beat us because they've been made aware which of <u>us</u> is being offered the scholarship.

> *(fear0000 and Ashworth1 look at each other [this wasn't disclosed], as MaMaLynn3 raises an eyebrow, trying not to react.)*

MaMaLynn3

And how can you be so sure?

> *(imcnu4ever pulls a document out of a folder or a briefcase or something.)*

imcnu4ever

(presenting evidence) This is a transcript of a text communication between the talent scout and The Lewisburg Lions' Healer's mother, who just so happens to attend the same middle-aged women's self-defense class as <u>my</u> mother.

Ashworth1

Your honour!

imcnu4ever

She saw the text. She reported it to me. Quote: "It was a pretty easy decision, honestly. That Captain's got a bright future ahead of <u>her</u>."

fear0000

(outraged) Your honour!

imcnu4ever

(case closed) Exactly. Your honour. <u>You're</u> being offered the scholarship. Which is why you <u>must</u> recuse yourself from the rest of these proceedings.

> *(Ashworth1 and fear0000 erupt into disgruntled mutterings, but they're not actually saying anything, they're just going 'Mubbah mumbah bumbah mubbbah' etc. MaMaLynn3 gives one final, definitive WHACK of the gavel, eliciting silence.)*

MaMaLynn3

(no longer British) You're right. I'm stepping down. *(to turtle-dance)* But there's still the matter of what to do with you….

fear0000

I'll take it from here.

h00ba_h00ba

All rise! This court is in session again. The right honorable Judge fear presiding.

> *(fear0000 dons her own robe and a Judge Judy-style bob, shooing MaMaLynn3 from the stand. MaMaLynn3 disrobes, joining imcnu4ever. Perhaps another musical sting covers the transition.)*

fear0000

(with some kind of stereotypical New Jersey dialect) Now. Quitcha moanin' and get ta ownin'. What's with the turtle?

turtle-dance

Wait, am I still on trial?

MaMaLynn3

(to turtle-dance) Shush. *(to fear0000)* Your honor. *(to the whole room)* Members of the court. I move that it's time to start training turtle-dance as a part of the team.

Ashworth1 *(overlapping)* Ooh!!
h00ba_h00ba *(overlapping)* What??
fear0000 *(overlapping)* Her??
turtle-dance *(overlapping)* Me??

fear0000

(wresting control without the gavel) Okay okay okay, shut it and butt it. *(to MaMaLynn3)* Why? If I may be so bold.

MaMaLynn3

Why?

fear0000

Why <u>now</u>? Why the sudden change of heart? Especially after the colossal screw up she committed on Saturday.

MaMaLynn3

I know. But she's waited long enough. She's a part of this team and she deserves to be treated as such. It's my fault that she hasn't seen any field time, and it's my responsibility to correct that mistake.

> *(fear0000 narrows her eyes suspiciously at MaMaLynn3.)*

fear0000

(dismissively) Nah. I don't buy it. Bailiff, get 'er outta here.

h00ba_h00ba
(moving to remove MaMaLynn3) With pleasure.

MaMaLynn3
No, no, it's true!

> *(MaMaLynn3 struggles against h00ba_h00ba as fear0000 continues. Ashworth1 provides some 'mubbah mubbah's again, maybe even trying to get turtle-dance to join in, but turtle-dance has no idea what's going on. imcnu4ever is distraught.)*

fear0000
Save it for ya cell mate. See if some time behind bars makes you a little more forthcomin'.

MaMaLynn3
(almost breaking out of the conceit) fear, I–!!

fear0000
Bailiff, get a move on!

Ashworth1
MUBBAH MUMBLE BUMBAH MUBBAH!!

turtle-dance
You guys are being so–!

imcnu4ever
(cutting through everything) MaMaLynn3 and I kissed. *(after the silence)* And I'm moving. To a new school.

(There is an abominable pause.)

imcnu4ever

Well. *(nothing happens)* Somebody render a verdict.

> *(h00ba_h00ba releases MaMaLynn3 and makes her way to replace fear0000.)*

h00ba_h00ba

I'll take this one.

> *(h00ba_h00ba dons her own robe and a pair of little glasses.)*

h00ba_h00ba

(rushing through this bit a bit) All rise the court is in session for a third time, the honorable Judge me presiding. *(having settled in; to imcnu4ever; with the deepest Southern drawl)* Now, I say, I say, now, where in tarnation do you get the gall…to come into my courtroom and assault us with a double-decker pig slaw sandwich of information such as what you have just done did here now?

imcnu4ever

My mom got a new job. We have to relocate by the end of the week. And kissing MaMaLynn3 was my choice, I–

h00ba_h00ba

Now, now, now, now, now we don't care…who you smooch around with in your free time. If anything, we're happy for you both.

fear0000

(more shocked than facetious, but just barely) Thrilled, actually.

h00ba_h00ba

What we care about is the fact that you're leavin' us higher
and drier than a mid-April cactus.

imcnu4ever

I'll spend this week training her. Then, you can destroy those
dirty-playing lions in my memory.

fear0000

Jeez, cnu. You make it sound so terminal.

Ashworth1

Yeah, I mean, you can stay in touch, can't you?

imcnu4ever

Why would I?

> *(The other Coyotes look at her. That's not the
> response they expected. h00ba_h00ba recovers
> enough to bang the gavel.)*

h00ba_h00ba

Overruled!

imcnu4ever

(defiant) Over-overruled!

fear0000

Double, super, extra, secret, triple overruled!!

imcnu4ever

You guys are being stupid.

fear0000

You're being stupid!! MaMaLynn3, make her stay!

(MaMaLynn3 can't make eye contact with anyone. She's already made her peace. Another migraine is brewing.)

Ashworth1

(a plea to imcnu4ever) But, we're Coyotes. *([that should be enough])*

imcnu4ever

I won't be. If my new school has a team, one day I might even play <u>against</u> you.

(No one likes the taste of that. h00ba_h00ba takes off her glasses and rises, dropping the judge routine.)

h00ba_h00ba

So, that's it? You're either with us or you're against us?

imcnu4ever

([that's what I said]) Yeah.

fear0000

Harsh.

imcnu4ever

What are you <u>talking</u> about? *(scoffs)* Every <u>day</u> in this room someone's saying "We're not friends, we're teammates." Soon we won't even be that. Of course it's harsh, but you all know how grueling this life is. When's the last time any of you took a whole weekend off? Slept in? Went on a date?

h00ba_h00ba

(defiant the whole way through) Alright, that's not fair, cause no one ever asks me on a date, wait, shut up, *(to the room)* let her finish!

imcnu4ever

We can <u>never</u> compromise. To be as good as we are, we have to eat, breathe, and dream this sport. I know you all do, and I'm not gonna stop either. So, <u>if</u> we meet each other again on the digital battlefield…I won't take it easy on any of you. I respect you all way too much for that. *([should she? yeah])* I love you all way too much for that.

> *(Everyone waits to see what's coming next. MaMaLynn3 decides.)*

MaMaLynn3

(extending a hand to imcnu4ever) It's good of you to take turtle-dance under your wing.

> *(imcnu4ever takes MaMaLynn3's hand in a martial handshake.)*

MaMaLynn3

And if she's half the Scout you are, your new team will be in trouble when next we meet.

> *(MaMaLynn3 and imcnu4ever smile at each other.)*

imcnu4ever

Court adjourned.

> *(h00ba_h00ba bangs the gavel and joins the rest of the group.)*

imcnu4ever

What'd'y'say, Captain? *(of turtle-dance)* Shall we let the pup off-leash?

(MaMaLynn3 turns to turtle-dance.)

MaMaLynn3

Well, kid? Are you ready to join the pack?

turtle-dance

(absolutely overcome, stumbling over herself) Yes! I mean—
Yes, of course. *(to imcnu4ever)* I'm so sorry you're leaving,
but— *(to the group)* If it's time to play I'm ready! I'm <u>so</u>
ready. Thank you.

MaMaLynn3

(to the group) Battlestations, Coyotes! We've got a rematch
to prepare for. fear, set it up.

fear0000

(begrudging, but excited) Aye, aye!

h00ba_h00ba

(just excited) Let's do it!

Ashworth1

(as she passes turtle-dance; genuinely) Congrats, girl.

> *(MaMaLynn3, h00ba_h00ba, fear0000,
> Ashworth1, and turtle-dance take to their
> battlestations, headsets on. imcnu4ever leans
> over turtle-dance's shoulder.)*

imcnu4ever

(to turtle-dance) Lemme see your load-out. *(points at the
screen)* Great, don't forget to up your durability ASAP.

> *(MaMaLynn3's migraine is really setting in. She
> clutches her temples with one hand, trying to
> stay focused on the screen ahead.)*

fear0000

Map's a go. Ready up?

Ashworth1

Locked and loaded.

h00ba_h00ba

Let's K some A. *(noticing)* MaMaLynn3, you with us?

(MaMaLynn3 shakes her head to clear it.)

MaMaLynn3

Yep. Ready up. I want a clear map so we can push the fortress from both sides. Ready?

imcnu4ever *(simultaneous)* Ready.
h00ba_h00ba *(simultaneous)* Ready.
Ashworth1 *(simultaneous)* Ready.
fear0000 *(simultaneous)* Ready.

(turtle-dance exhales.)

turtle-dance

Ready.

MaMaLynn3

Coyotes. Let's play!

*(The Coyotes all lean in. The sound of clicking
and keyboards and the game fill the space. The
lights fade on The Coyotes' intense focus. After
the lights have gone out, the soundscape fades
away.)*

SCENE SIX – TUESDAY – TALKIN' WITH TURTLE-DANCE™

The Coyotes are at their battlestations post-practice. They are in nearly-identical positions to the day before. They have been playing intensely and, as the lights come up, they exhale and lean back in their seats.

h00ba_h00ba

(ripping off her headphones) Heck yeeeaaaahhhhh!

(Ashworth1 takes off her headphones, rises, and high-fives turtle-dance.)

Ashworth1

Not too shabby!!

imcnu4ever

(to turtle-dance) Better than yesterday. You catch on quick.

MaMaLynn3

(she almost can't believe it) I'll say. We've never beaten Lava Junction so quickly.

fear0000

Looks like you're a real upgrade, turtle. *(realizing)* I mean–

MaMaLynn3

([it's not fine]) It's fine.

fear0000

Yeah. *(to turtle-dance)* You're fine.

MaMaLynn3

Let's call it a day. Great work, Coyotes. Katie, do you wanna…?

imcnu4ever

Yeah, I do.

fear0000

(suggestively, to whomever's near) Yeah, they do.

MaMaLynn3

(to fear0000) Zip it. *(to the group)* Dismissed. See you tomorrow.

> *(The Coyotes gather their things and chat as they depart. h00ba_h00ba, MaMaLynn3, imcnu4ever, and fear0000 exit through the SR door. turtle-dance stops Ashworth1 briefly.)*

turtle-dance

Hey, Rebecca, uh, can we talk?

Ashworth1

"Rebecca?" Ooh, now I feel like I'm in trouble.

turtle-dance

No, I just–...I wanted to ask about...the team.

Ashworth1

I mean, you're definitely a part of it now, so...ask away.

turtle-dance

I was just curious about the...way things are? Around here sometimes?

Ashworth1

Oh, the smell? *(checking to make sure h00ba_h00ba isn't in earshot)* Yeah, I thought that was h00ba at first too, but it <u>is</u> the room. Mr. Derrick says there's nothing // they can do about that.

turtle-dance

No, no, no, no, no, not the smell. I've gotten used to that. It's more the…vibe. Or rather…the vibe<u>s</u>.

Ashworth1

How do you mean?

turtle-dance

MaMaLynn3 and h00ba get mad at each other and it's not a catfight; it's a gunfight at the OMG Coral. You guys literally went primal when you found out about the talent scout, and no one batted an eye.

Ashworth1

Mmmm, I don't think I follow.

turtle-dance

Yesterday? The courtroom drama? Doesn't it just feel sometimes like things get a little…

Ashworth1

A little…?

turtle-dance

You know. A little…

> *(Suddenly, it's a late night talk show. The theme song plays! A desk is pushed on from SL and in front of turtle-dance. The desk says "Talkin' with turtle-dance™." A coffee mug is put in turtle-*

*dance's hand, and a chair knocks into the back
of her legs, making her sit behind the desk. A
plush chair is pushed on from SR, which scoops
up Ashworth1 very naturally. She takes a
comfortable position and waits for the
conversation to continue. The scene is set:
turtle-dance is the host, Ashworth1 is the guest.)*

turtle-dance

(looking around at what just happened) Weird.

(A mug is brought to Ashworth1.)

Ashworth1

(pleasantly) Oh. *(mouthing)* Thank you. *(to turtle-dance)*
You were saying?

turtle-dance

Like *(gesturing at the change)* this. I just wanted to have a
conversation. Why has everything suddenly become a
spectacle?

Ashworth1

(an immaculate guest) Great question. But if there's one
thing the Coyotes know, it's that you can't spell spectacle
without being this <u>spectacular</u>!

*(There is an audience reaction of cheers and
laughter.)*

turtle-dance

I don't–… That's not wh–... *(searching around her)* And
where is that // applause coming from?

Ashworth1

Is that a question for me or did you want to keep interviewing the gum under your desk?

(Another reaction, lots of laughter.)

turtle-dance

I'm sorry, I–

Ashworth1

Hey, can I make an observation? This doesn't seem to be your…how can I put this? Natural element. *(gasp)* Oh my god, am I your first guest?

turtle-dance

What are you <u>talking</u> about?

Ashworth1

You know what? We're gonna be right back after a word from our sponsors.

(Music plays and the stage is swarmed with deckhands. They facilitate the transition of moving turtle-dance into the SR guest chair and setting Ashworth1 up behind the desk. The branding on the front of the desk is changed to say Ashworth1 After Dark™. Ashworth1's hair and makeup is touched up. The final adjustment is that their mugs are taken away and replaced with identical mugs. Now, Ashworth1 is the host, and very comfortably so, and turtle-dance is the tentative guest. Ashworth1 gestures and the music cuts out.)

Ashworth1

(oozing charisma) And we're back! With a really exciting
guest, the newest addition to the Coyote Thunder frontline,
give it up for turtle-dance!

> *(The audience applauds. Perhaps an 'Applause'*
> *sign even lights up, or someone enters with a*
> *sign that reads 'Applause.')*

Ashworth1

So, turtle-dance. You've just been officially promoted from
Swing to Scout. How are you feeling? Must be a lot of
adrenaline competing with the usual assortment of
hormones.

turtle-dance

Yyyyyeah, it's a lot, but…it's what I wanted, so–

Ashworth1

(the ultimate girl's girl) And why wouldn't you? You're so
good! Is it true you cleared half the Doomsweep map in less
than ten minutes on your <u>first</u> <u>try</u>?

(The crowd Oohs and Aahs.)

turtle-dance

You know I did. That was yesterday. You were there.

Ashworth1

Mhm, mhm. And what's this I hear about you not getting the
"vibe" around here?

turtle-dance

It just seems like every day there's a new…I dunno, bit? That I'm not always clued into? I don't want to say it's <u>weird</u>, but…it's kind of weird. And, I dunno, I feel like sometimes it can be a distraction or a deflection or–…

Ashworth1

And hey, I get that. It's that kind of honest, unfiltered talk that keeps us on the air. That and our sponsorship from Red Bull, am I right?

(Ashworth1 and the crowd laugh.)

Ashworth1

(back to it) No, we don't actually have a sponsorship with Red Bull, but what we <u>do</u> have is six, now five, young ladies who are in the most crucial and formative years of their lives. A group of performers and digital athletes who are chipping away at the glass ceiling underneath the feet of a male-dominated sport in a male-dominated field in a male-dominated world.

(The crowd gives an uproar of approval.)

turtle-dance

So our answer to that is playing pretend?

Ashworth1

(getting a little more serious) "Playing pretend?" In prize money <u>alone</u>, the current lifetime earnings of the highest-paid female esports athlete is four hundred and seventy-two thousand dollars. That's not a bad slice of pie for "playing pretend."

turtle-dance

That's not what I meant.

Ashworth1

(driving home the point) It's also <u>nothing</u> compared to the highest-paid <u>male</u> esports player as of this year – a whopping seven point two <u>million</u> in lifetime earnings.

turtle-dance

I'm not talking about money.

Ashworth1

And neither am I. Not really. Listen, the scholarship's a very exciting motivator, but between you, me, and the studio audience, I'm not going to school for Boneblood Arena 2. My parents would kill me.

> *(Murmurs of agreement and understanding from the crowd. Ashworth1 quells the rumblings a little bit.)*

Ashworth1

Now, that doesn't mean I'm not all boneblood, bonesweat, and bonetears in the meantime. But the money really just symbolizes respect. Take the Harlington High Panthers, for example. You know them?

> *(The audience clamors and murmurs [we don't like them].)*

turtle-dance

I know <u>of</u> them.

Ashworth1

The Lions are one thing. But the Panthers? Those guys are <u>intentionally</u> boys-only.

turtle-dance

Aren't we girls-only?

Ashworth1

(chuckling) <u>No</u>! We just happen to be right now. Coyote Thunder was started by boys <u>and</u> girls, before your time, before mine. This just so happens to be the, pun intended, makeup of the team right now.

(The audience laughs a little; it was a fine joke.)

Ashworth1

My point is, The Panthers go out of their <u>way</u> to be exclusionary. And where do they learn that behavior? From the adults around them. From the history of the industry. And from no one telling them to do otherwise.

(The audience agrees.)

turtle-dance

So what are you saying? The system's unjust, let's all pretend to be cowboys?

(Ashworth1 rises from the desk and moves downstage, facing the audience, giving her end-of-show monologue.)

Ashworth1

What I'm <u>saying</u>, dear sweet turtle-dance, is that you can get into this industry for a lot of reasons. You can do it for money, but you're never gonna break the bank. You can do it for love, but you're only gonna break your heart. Or you can do it for <u>fun</u>. And if it's supposed to be fun, why not let it be as much fun as our little bodies can handle? You say "weird?" I say <u>inspired</u>. <u>Inventive</u>. Does it feel <u>silly</u> to get into an argument with MaMaLynn3 and suddenly realize

Ashworth1 (cont)

we've been hissing at each other like vampires for twenty minutes? *(chuckling at the memory)* You betcha. But I tell you what: it beats the hell out of worrying what other people are gonna think. If I can laugh at myself, if I can take myself a little less seriously…nothing they can do can hurt me. If the world isn't going to take care of us, if the world isn't going to make <u>room</u> for us, then we have a responsibility to create worlds that will.

> *(turtle-dance is very moved by this. She's starting to get it. She rises and starts to speak.)*

turtle-dance

I–

> *(The talk show's outro sting starts to play.)*

Ashworth1

But that's our show, folks. Gents, gals, and non-binary pals, thanks so much for tuning in *(pointing to the audience)* whether you're live in here *(pointing to her heart)* or you live in here. We'll see you next time. Goodnight!

> *(The music swells. Ashworth1 moves back and approaches turtle-dance, shaking her hand and mouthing thanks and congratulations. They have a bit more back and forth, but we can't hear what they're saying, as if the credits were rolling over them. The furniture gets moved away and off. Ashworth1 gestures upstage right and she and turtle-dance move offstage together, not through the door. Blackout.)*

<u>**SCENE SEVEN – WEDNESDAY – WALK THE PLANK**</u>

> *MaMaLynn3, fear0000, Ashworth1, and h00ba_h00ba are pirates, hooting, arr-ing, and celebrating. h00ba_h00ba has a concertina (or similar instrument), Ashworth1 has an eyepatch, and fear0000 is passing around a bottle of "ale." They are all wearing tricorn hats.*

fear0000

O, cap'n, me cap'n. Wet yer whistle with a swig-a this! Nothin'll cure whatever ails you better than…well…ale!

> *(turtle-dance enters through the SR door as fear0000 passes the bottle to MaMaLynn3. MaMaLynn3 drinks deep.)*

turtle-dance

Hey, sorry I'm– *(seeing the bottle; somewhere between a shout and a whisper)* Are you guys drinking?!

> *(Ashworth1 leans toward turtle-dance and lifts her eye patch.)*

Ashworth1

(sotto voce) It's sparkling apple juice, relax. *(lowering her eye patch)* Ya har.

turtle-dance

Oh. *(trying)* Yar.

h00ba_h00ba

Our fearless leader was just regaling us with how she found herself ensconced in the arms of her fair, bonny lassie.

turtle-dance

How she what?

fear0000

(exasperated) Ugh! MaMaLynn3 and cnu went on their first date last night and she was just about to tell us the juicy details. Will you get with the program? *(back to pirate)* Ya har!

turtle-dance

Oh! That's great. Um…ya har!

> *(fear0000, h00ba_h00ba, and Ashworth1 echo turtle-dance's 'Ya har.')*

h00ba_h00ba

Tell us the tale, captain! Be not so stoic a sea dog as to speak no dead man's tales.

MaMaLynn3

Alright, ye bilge rats. Then lend a salty ear.

> *(h00ba_h00ba begins playing the concertina, or a recording makes it seem so.)*

MaMaLynn3

There I was…she and I…I and she…docked in the harbor of the Red Lobster.

Ashworth1

The one by the mall?

MaMaLynn3

Nay. *(with a suggestive wink)* The nice one.

> *(Ashworth1 and fear0000 react with joy at this revelation.)*

h00ba_h00ba
(singing a sea shanty)
"She and I, and I and she,
In the parking lot off I-70!"

MaMaLynn3
I looked deep into her eyes. They blazed like the sun through a morning squall. And in that moment I knew, no treasure nor jewel could rival what sweetness sparkled there.

h00ba_h00ba
(singing)
No chest full of gold nor glittering share
Could match the bright love that I saw buried there!"

MaMaLynn3
I leaned in. Hoping to taste a drop of paradise upon those perfect lips. But before I could set my course toward that blessed shore, she stopped me.

fear0000
Blast!

Ashworth1
A torture most sweet!

h00ba_h00ba
(singing)
"Heavenly lips sink ships.
Beware the roll of the lady's hips!"

MaMaLynn3
She swore to me that though her voyage might take her across the horizon, she would remain faithful. And that if I were to send her regular missives, she would reply in kind.

Ashworth1

And what then, cap'n? Did she send you home wanting?

fear0000

Did she abandon ye adrift on a lonely sea?

MaMaLynn3

(with a wicked grin) Ohhhh no. We swore our oaths to one another time and time again. *(with another wink and a nudge)* For ye know how spacious the backseat of a 2019 Honda Civic can be!

(MaMaLynn3, Ashworth1, fear0000, and h00ba_h00ba give a devilish laugh.)

Ashworth1

And she swore to be true?

MaMaLynn3

To me and me alone!

fear0000

How do you feel?

MaMaLynn3

Like the king of the seas!

turtle-dance

(trying her gosh-darnedest) Did y'plunder her treasure chest, cap'n?

(The concertina squawks to a stop. The other Coyotes gawp at turtle-dance. MaMaLynn3 rises, a heat in her eyes.)

MaMaLynn3

Did I plunder her <u>what</u>, sailor?

turtle-dance

(terrified and small) H–her, her treasure chest?

MaMaLynn3

(advancing on turtle-dance) You would ask of the woman I love whether I sullied her most-perfect self with my profaned touch?

(*turtle-dance gulps and nods.*)

MaMaLynn3

Well…not only did I so… *(suddenly elated; she was messing with turtle-dance)* But I also got my hands on her booty!

(*The Coyotes give a raucous cheer. It's a celebration once more! The concertina begins again, and The Coyotes sing a sea shanty.*)

ALL

(singing)
"Me hearties are hardy wherever they roam.
They keep me afloat when me vessel's from home.
And though nights are lonely, I'll never lose heart,
For Coyote Thunder will ne'er grow apart!
No, Coyote Thunder will ne'er grow aparrrrtttt!"

(*The Coyotes fall about laughing. The pirate aesthetic fades away, as do their props, except for the bottle, which h00ba_h00ba keeps and takes another swig from. They're just high school girls again, laughing and enjoying one another's company.*)

Ashworth1

Wow. *(of imcnu4ever)* I'm really gonna miss her. *(to MaMaLynn3)* And I know you are too.

MaMaLynn3

You wanna know the funny thing?

fear0000

What?

MaMaLynn3

She's not even moving that far away. It's another school district, but she's only going to Meekerville.

h00ba_h00ba

That's like a forty-minute drive!

(MaMaLynn3 smiles and nods. The Coyotes burst into laughter once more. The joy is infectious. Some tears might spring from it. Even a howl or two. They sigh, they relax. The pirate aesthetic is gone, but they're still a crew. They dwell for a moment and then, for MaMaLynn3 at least, the melancholy sinks in. Thunder rolls in the distance. The lights fade as the storm swells. Lightning. Then darkness.)

<u>**SCENE EIGHT – THURSDAY – AVM**</u>
> *Mr. Derrick is on. h00ba_h00ba, Ashworth1,*
> *fear0000, and turtle-dance enter mid-*
> *conversation.*

h00ba_h00ba

(continuing a story from offstage) And I said, "You tell me, it's <u>your</u> toothbrush."

fear0000

I can't tell if that's a terrible joke or if you're just bad at telling it.

Ashworth1

Hey, Mr. Derrick, // what's up?

fear0000

Ew, Derrick. What are you doing here?

Mr. Derrick

Hey, guys. Sorry to interrupt your practice but, uh. We need to talk.

Ashworth1

Have you seen MaMaLynn3? She wasn't in last period.

Mr. Derrick

She's not here, –

fear0000

Yeah, no duh. Thanks for the timely news, Pony Express. So is practice // cancelled or–?

Mr. Derrick

That's–… *(the adult in the room at last; not harsh but firm)* Okay, you guys should sit down.

(The Coyotes catch the shift. They sit at their stations.)

turtle-dance

What happened?

Mr. Derrick

Uh. Okay, so. I just got off the phone with all your parents. Principal Delk had me call them, and they all thought it would be alright for you to hear it from me. They'll talk to you about it more when you get home, but um… Lynne passed away this morning. Those…headaches she got–

Ashworth1

Her migraines.

Mr. Derrick

Yeah. They weren't just migraines. She had a… *(reaches into his pocket; pulls out a piece of paper)* Sorry, I had to write this down. Uh, she had an AVM. It has to do with the blood vessels in her brain. It's nothing that– I mean, she was born with it but. There was nothing to be done. She went to sleep last night and she just…never woke up.

fear0000

Oh my god.

Mr. Derrick

We told Katie's parents too. They were already on the road, so it's not ideal but…she knows. *(when no one responds)* Um. We just found out after school, so the counselor and the nurse have both gone home, but. I'm here, the principal's here, if you need to talk. Or you can go home and talk about it with your families. I think some of your parents are on their way to pick you up.

(No one speaks. No one moves. They're all struggling to breathe.)

Mr. Derrick

I know this is hard. Harder than…anything you should have to experience at this age. I know she was your friend.

h00ba_h00ba

No, she wasn't.

(Mr. Derrick, Ashworth1, fear0000, and turtle-dance all turn to stare at her.)

h00ba_h00ba

She wasn't our <u>friend</u>. She was more than that. She was our <u>teammate</u>.

Mr. Derrick

(he doesn't get it but he gets it) Yeah. So. I'm gonna let you guys process. Just come check in with me before you leave, okay?

Ashworth1

(numb) We will, Mr. Derrick.

Mr. Derrick

Okay.

(Mr. Derrick leaves, closing the door behind him. The Coyotes sit in silence for a moment.)

turtle-dance

What do we do?

h00ba_h00ba

(putting on her headphones) We practice.

fear000

What?

h00ba_h00ba

Ready up. Lava Gulch. Gold bots on. Let's go.

turtle-dance

I don't think we should–

h00ba_h00ba

(a wounded animal) I SAID READY UP!! MaMa was the Tank when I joined the team and then she became the Captain. Well, I was the Tank and now she's gone so I'm the Captain, and you'll respect that like you would have respected her, got it??

> *(turtle-dance reels for a moment. Then she nods and puts on her headphones. Ashworth1 and fear0000 do the same.)*

h00ba_h00ba

Ready up? Three. Two. One.

> *(The game starts, and The Coyotes, what's left of them, play in silence. After a few moments of mouse clicks and keyboard clacks, a voice buzzes in over the intercom.)*

Voice

(offstage) Grace Hubert, Rebecca Ashworth, and Jade Lee, please come to the front office for dismissal.

SCENE NINE – FRIDAY – TO BE OR NOT TO BE?

The room is a mausoleum. Dark, candlelit. Hushed whispers or chanted hymns echo off the stone walls. Three hooded figures enter; they are h00ba_h00ba, Ashworth1, and fear0000. They are druids or witches. The ritual begins.

fear0000

Our leader has fallen.

Ashworth1

Taken before her time.

h00ba_h00ba

But her spirit can be avenged.

Ashworth1

<u>Must</u> be avenged.

fear0000

<u>Will</u> be avenged.

(h00ba_h00ba, Ashworth1, and fear0000 raise their instruments solemnly. turtle-dance enters through the door SR.)

turtle-dance

(frustrated) Guys.

Ashworth1

Speak our enemy's name.

h00ba_h00ba *(simultaneously)* A. V. M.
fear0000 *(simultaneously)* A. V. M.

Ashworth1

And give its name meaning.

h00ba_h00ba

A vile monster.

fear0000

A vicious murderer.

turtle-dance

Guys, can we not do this? It was an aneurysm. Not some bad guy you can beat up.

fear0000

We need not conquer the AVM.

Ashworth1

Only death itself.

turtle-dance

Ah yeah, much more rational response.

h00ba_h00ba

We deny you, death, your taken prize! We command our Lynne once more to rise!!

turtle-dance

Okay, you guys have officially been playing too many video games.

(turtle-dance flicks on the light switch. h00ba_h00ba, Ashworth1, and fear0000 hiss and flinch away from the light.)

h00ba_h00ba

You rob us of our ritual!

turtle-dance

This is <u>not</u> the way to handle this.

fear0000

(to Ashworth1 and h00ba_h00ba, of turtle-dance) She thinks she knows a better path to immortality.

Ashworth1

If she knows a way to preserve the den mother's memory, speak it now!

turtle-dance

If you want to memorialize her, fine. But also, like, go to therapy or something.

fear0000

(excited) A sacrifice??

turtle-dance

That's not what I said at all.

Ashworth1

You know not the extent of our suffering. None knew her as we did.

turtle-dance

I don't know if that's entirely fair. You guys knew her longer than I did, sure, but <u>plenty</u> of people are grieving. Her family, the school…

Ashworth1

They matter not! The mother's memory demands tribute!

h00ba_h00ba

Pain!

fear0000

Despair!

Ashworth1

Let her name be thundered!

fear0000 *(simultaneous)* MaMaLynn3! MaMaLynn3!
h00ba_h00ba *(simultaneous)* MaMaLynn3! MaMaLynn3!

Ashworth1

Weaken our spirits and strike at our souls that her legacy
may last forever!!

> *(Ashworth1 howls as fear0000 and
> h00ba_h00ba continue to chant MaMaLynn3's
> name. Eventually, they begin to devolve into a
> ritualistic spectacle, self-flagellating, writhing
> on the ground. They are keening, mourning,
> overwhelmed with their sorrow and anguish.
> There is no comfort in their minds, and their
> cacophony rises, overwhelming turtle-dance.)*

turtle-dance

Stop it! Stop it!! Why are you doing this?? What do you
think this is accomplishing?? Why can't you all just be
normal???

> *(h00ba_h00ba, fear0000, and Ashworth1 fall
> into huddled prayer positions on the ground,
> their hooded robes covering them completely as
> if they weren't there. MaMaLynn3 enters from a
> direction no one has entered from yet.)*

MaMaLynn3

Is it hurting anyone?

turtle-dance

Lynne!

MaMaLynn3

Hello, friend. Sorry for the abrupt entrance. And the abrupt exit.

turtle-dance

Are you…a ghost?

MaMaLynn3

[(how to explain?)] No, I'm…a manifestation of your repressed imagination.

turtle-dance

My–?

MaMaLynn3

(not an accusation, just a fact) You're no fun.

turtle-dance

What??

MaMaLynn3

Sorry. Sorry. That is…not what I meant. Not what <u>you</u> meant. What <u>we</u> meant was…what's the harm in playing a little?

turtle-dance

I already did this interview with Ashworth.

MaMaLynn3

Doesn't look like it stuck.

75

turtle-dance

I've tried to join in!

MaMaLynn3

Emphasis on <u>tried</u>.

turtle-dance

I did the finger guns! And the pirate stuff! And–and the zombie thing! I tried so–, I really. I thought the zombie thing was a good offering, even though it felt <u>so</u> <u>stupid</u>.

MaMaLynn3

(meaning The Coyotes) When they play, they don't feel stupid. They're just having fun.

turtle-dance

(observing the ground around her) This is <u>fun</u> to them?

MaMaLynn3

It's more fun than shutting down. Or bottling it up. Or taking it out on someone else.

turtle-dance

It's not healthy!

MaMaLynn3

Yeah, well! You wanna eat carrots every day of your life, or you wanna have a little cake from time to time?

turtle-dance

How am I even having this argument with myself?

MaMaLynn3

What do you mean?

turtle-dance

I know what I think. But if you're coming from my subconscious, why am I trying to convince <u>myself</u> of something I don't believe?

MaMaLynn3

Sounds like on some level you do believe it.

turtle-dance

That doesn't make any sense.

MaMaLynn3

No fun <u>and</u> stubborn. What a winning combo.

turtle-dance

Apparently I'm a little rude too.

MaMaLynn3

You should get a better outlet.

turtle-dance

Every time I tried to play along, they looked at me like I had three heads.

MaMaLynn3

First of all, that would have been a lot of fun. Not sure what genre to stick it in; maybe a mutant, wasteland, post-apocalyptic kinda thing–

turtle-dance

Focus.

MaMaLynn3

Second, it's because you weren't actually doing what they were doing. You were trying to do what they were doing "right."

turtle-dance

What do you mean? What do…<u>I</u> mean?

MaMaLynn3

How much do you think these girls actually know about cowboys? Or pirates? Or 1930s gangsters?

turtle-dance

Surface level, I imagine.

MaMaLynn3

And yet, they dive in with their whole hearts. They're not afraid of getting it right or wrong, they just want to play. They don't want to "fit in" so…they fit in. With each other.

turtle-dance

Sounds easier thought than done.

MaMaLynn3

You <u>can</u> do it. You have the same stuff in you that they do.

turtle-dance

How?

MaMaLynn3

Do you really want to know?

turtle-dance

Would you be here if I didn't?

MaMaLynn3

(smiles) Touché. There's hope for you yet, turtle-dance.

turtle-dance

So what do I do?

MaMaLynn3

I can only walk you there if you're willing to hold your own
hand.

turtle-dance

(considers; decides) I am.

MaMaLynn3

Okay. Stand like this.

> *(MaMaLynn3 stands with one foot forward in a
> sort of modified third position. turtle-dance
> takes the same stance.)*

turtle-dance

Like this?

MaMaLynn3

Mm-hm. Hand up.

> *(MaMaLynn3 holds up her dominant hand as if
> she were holding Yorick's skull, a very
> traditional Shakespearean pose.)*

turtle-dance

Okay.

MaMaLynn3

Chin up a bit.

> *(turtle-dance raises her chin.)*

turtle-dance

Now what?

MaMaLynn3

Now comes what's called an ecphonesis. It's usually written as the letter "O", but in our Shakespeare class, Mrs. Johnson says it's "The sound your soul makes when words just aren't enough." You must have overheard that at some point.

turtle-dance

You want me to do that?

MaMaLynn3

(shrugs) <u>You</u> do. On some level.

turtle-dance

It's too silly.

MaMaLynn3

Then die a serious person.

turtle-dance

Ouch.

MaMaLynn3

Hey, <u>I</u> didn't. I'm the epitome of "To thine own self be true." *(over the back of her hand, as if sharing a secret)* Hamlet, act one, scene three. You'll thank me Junior year.

turtle-dance

Stop it. I can't know that if I don't know it, and if I already knew it you're not telling me anything I don't know.

MaMaLynn3

Wow, maybe you can't do it. Maybe you can't just let go and play in the moment.

turtle-dance

I play when I play the game. My life is my life.

MaMaLynn3

Your life <u>is</u> a game. And you're the main character. Start acting like it.

turtle-dance

By pretending to be something else?

MaMaLynn3

Yes! For a start.

turtle-dance

I can't, okay? I thought I could, but I can't.

MaMaLynn3

Why not?

turtle-dance

I'm scared!

MaMaLynn3

Of what?

turtle-dance

Of people thinking I'm weird!

MaMaLynn3

What people?

turtle-dance

Anyone! Everyone! Strangers! Friends!

MaMaLynn3

And what will happen if they think you're weird?

turtle-dance

I don't know! I'm just–

MaMaLynn3

What?

turtle-dance

Scared!!

MaMaLynn3

Of what??

turtle-dance

Fear!

MaMaLynn3

Let it out!

turtle-dance

I can't!

MaMaLynn3

You have to, Coyote!

turtle-dance

I don't know how!

MaMaLynn3

Yes, you do! Just stop thinking and do it. YOU HAVE TO
COMMUNICATE!

> *(turtle-dance's ecphonesis is large and
> cathartic.)*

turtle-dance

O!

O, that my fears were foes in battle faced!
That I might meet them, toe-to-toe in solemn stride
And know that either they or I must fall,
But to be done; to put an end to them or me.
But fear is not my foe; it is an armor.
I wrap it 'round myself like arms of fire
That none may touch me, lest they sense my shake.
I forge myself against each daily world,
'Gainst bullying, rejection, doubt, and pain,
Some slights perceived and some imaginéd,
Letting my life wall about me so that
None may enter. And if none enter, none may harm.
And if none harm, I am alone. And if
I am alone, I am safe, but alone.
To be alive is to be home to pain,
To welcome it with open-arm'd embrace,
For as without the night there is no day,
Pain's absence cannot be known without pain.
Then what fear I but what will always be?
The sun will rise, and hurt will find my heart.
But surely as that same bright sun will set,
My heart will heal and will find peace again.
Then let me not an island make myself,
When in the tides of life such dolphins swim.
Rather, a ship, my sails tattered but full,
Let me become, on joyful waves to skim.
I need not fear when fear's a natural thing.
Instead I'll live, play, hope, laugh, cry, dance, sing.

*(MaMaLynn3 has exited during turtle-dance's
soliloquy. As it ends, turtle-dance dissolves into
tears. fear0000, h00ba_h00ba, and Ashworth1
rise and shed their robes as if they were never
wearing them and rush to comfort her.)*

fear0000

It's okay. You're okay.

turtle-dance

I can't believe she's gone.

h00ba_h00ba

Me neither.

turtle-dance

You're right, I didn't know her like you guys did… Why am I going to miss her so much?

Ashworth1

She was easy to love.

fear0000

She was a hell of a player.

h00ba_h00ba

A hell of a friend.

fear0000

Yeah. That too.

turtle-dance

Thank you. For not pushing me away. For not giving up on me.

> *(No one knows what to say, so they don't. They just smile and nod a bit.)*

h00ba_h00ba

So. What now?

fear0000

We should…practice? East Marsh is next week.

Ashworth1

God, and if The Lions still want a rematch, we'll have to find a fifth.

h00ba_h00ba

Who cares? None of us is getting the scholarship anyway.

fear0000

Ugh, we have so much work to do.

turtle-dance

Or we could just play.

(A small beat.)

h00ba_h00ba

How is that different?

turtle-dance

(holds her hand over her mouth to help do a deep announcer voice) In a world where the love of the game has been overshadowed by ruthless competition, one Coyote is doing what they never thought possible…finishing the story mode.

(The other Coyotes laugh and join in.)

fear0000

(holds her hand over her mouth to do a nasal voice) Coyotes, your mission, if you choose to accept it, is to download the mod that turns all the enemies into members of One Direction. *{this can be adjusted to whatever group is popular enough to be well-known but not so popular that most of the audience wouldn't enjoy that mod}*

Ashworth1

This missive will self-destruct.

(h00ba_h00ba jumps into the group, making a big explosion noise with her mouth. They're playing.)

h00ba_h00ba

You're totally right. There's only two months of school left. We don't have a Captain, so we're not going to qualifiers.

fear0000

We'll find some fresh blood and kick the pants off those Lions next year.

Ashworth1

I could use a break. Plus, the smell is starting to get a lot weirder.

(turtle-dance moves up to the battlestations and turns off her monitor.)

turtle-dance

In the meantime, maybe it's time to do…something else. I hear the drama club's looking for some last-minute understudies.

(h00ba_h00ba makes a face and shakes her head. Ashworth1 considers.)

fear0000

Not if you paid me. *(moves to her station and turns off her monitor)* But a break sounds nice. Time to read a book, watch a movie.

h00ba_h00ba

(moves to her station and turns off her monitor) Get out of this room. Go on a date.

(Ashworth1 moves to her station and turns off her monitor.)

Ashworth1

Go for a drive. *(turns off imcnu4ever's monitor)* Visit a friend.

(None of them can bring themselves to approach MaMaLynn3's battlestation.)

turtle-dance

And when we're ready, we can come back. Play again. And see what it's like after some time off. The real question is. Will the game be ready for us? Will they be able to handle the map-clearin'-est–

fear0000

–no fearin'-est–

h00ba_h00ba

–game so good you'll shed a tearin'-est–

Ashworth1

–<u>your</u> favorite esports team <u>and</u> mine…

(The lights become that of a stadium entrance as in the first scene. turtle-dance produces a microphone and takes center.)

turtle-dance

COYOTEEEEEEEEEEEE THUNNNNNDERRRRRRR!

(The Coyotes howl. Blackout. Silence. MaMaLynn3's monitor remains lit in the space

*for a moment, then goes out. Music and lights
blare for curtain call.)*

END